This book belongs to:

[Daddy]

and

[Me]

First published in Great Britain in 2019 by Seven Dials
an imprint of The Orion Publishing Group Ltd
Carmelite House, 50 Victoria Embankment
London EC4Y 0DZ

An Hachette UK Company

1 3 5 7 9 10 8 6 4 2

Copyright © Orion Publishing Group 2019
Written by Rebecca Meldrum

A CIP catalogue record for this book is
available from the British Library

ISBN: 9781841883724

Printed in Italy by Printer Trento

www.orionbooks.co.uk

Daddy and Me

An Activity Book

Rebecca Meldrum

SEVEN DIALS

Introduction

Memory-making with children is something that all parents do every day, but being able to make memories and capture them at the same time is seriously special! Dads can sometimes get overlooked when it comes to drawing and colouring with the kids so this book is especially for you - to help you carve out time to spend together as well as giving you the space to record those moments, either winding down after school, or perhaps on a rainy day when you're all stuck inside.

Some of you might already know me from watching my YouTube channel or following me on my social media platforms. If you don't then hello! It's lovely to meet you. I'm Rebecca: a mum, wife and lifestyle and parenting vlogger, sharing daily trials and tribulations on my YouTube channel - I'd love to chat to you over there. My followers are mostly mums and we'd love to add some lovely dads to the club so look me up, either on YouTube (www.youtube.com/user/MrsRMeldrum) or Instagram (@mrsrmeldrum).

More than anything I'd love to see you how you decide to use the book with your little ones, so do share on your social media channels if you're so inclined with the hashtag #daddyandmebook.

How to use the book

Use the book however you like - go wild! This book is all about memory-making, so don't be afraid of the pages: they are there to be doodled on, coloured in and enjoyed together. My little ones and I have gone hell for leather in my first book, *Mummy and Me*, and I know they'll be doing the same with their dad in this one - and that's really the point of the book. Start in the middle, flick back and forth, just use it however works for you. Some of the pages will take five minutes to fill in, some will take twenty-five or even longer, so pick whatever page suits you when you sit down to it: save it for special times or use it as a boredom buster.

On each page you'll find a prompt or activity, with a page for you dads to fill in on the left and your children to fill in on the right. You'll also see there's space for you to fill the date in and your little one to fill in their age - so that when they're all grown up you can look back through the book and see what you were both thinking and doing when they were little. This book is perfect to enjoy with children aged roughly 4-6 upwards. Some of the pages will require a little more help from you, but there are lots of activities you can complete with even littler ones too.

Most of the activities only require a pen or some colouring pencils to complete, but a few might ask for some extra bits and bobs: nothing that shouldn't already be in or around your home and you definitely don't have to be a crafty Pinterest Dad to enjoy it!

I never got very far with the baby memory books for my three girls because they were so pristine and beautiful that I didn't want to ruin them, whereas I hope this is more usable: something you can both put your stamp on and not be afraid of doing so! And I hope it helps you to create some really lovely memories together, that you can then treasure forever.

Lots of Love

Rebecca x

Here are some stars in the night sky. Join them up however you like to make your own constellation.

Daddy

DATE:

Here are some stars in the night sky. Join them up however you like to make your own constellation.

Me

If you were washed up on a desert island and you were allowed to take five items with you, what would they be?

Daddy

DATE:

If you were washed up on a desert island and you were allowed to take five items with you, what would they be?

Me

AGE

Colour these vegetables in using the WRONG colours.

Daddy

DATE:

Colour these vegetables in using
the WRONG colours.

AGE:

If a genie gave you three wishes, what would they be?

DATE:

If a genie gave you three wishes, what would they be?

AGE:

Birthday memories!

How old were you on your last birthday?

....

What did you do on your birthday?

....

Did you have a birthday party? If yes, what did you do?

....

Did you get any presents? What were they?

....

Did you have a cake? If yes, what kind?

....

Who did you celebrate with?

....

DATE:

Birthday memories!

How old were you on your last birthday?

....

What did you do on your birthday?

....

Did you have a birthday party? If yes, what did you do?

....

Did you get any presents? What were they?

....

Did you have a cake? If yes, what kind?

....

Who did you celebrate with?

....

Me

AGE:

Daddy

When Daddy was little

Time to get your little helper to interview you about what you got up to when you were younger! Ask them to read you the questions and then they can write in your answers.

What were you good at in school?

....

What was your favourite band?

....

Did you like to play any sports?

....

What did you do after school?

....

What did you want to be when you grew up?

....

Did you have to do any chores?

....

Did you get pocket money? If yes, how much?

....

Who was your best friend?

....

Me

AGE:

Draw each other a picture.

Daddy

DATE:

Draw each other a picture.

AGE:

Here's your own boat -
give it a name and write down
where you're going to sail it to.

Daddy

DATE:

Here's your own boat -
give it a name and write down
where you're going to sail it to.

Me

When was the last time you . . .

Had a haircut?

....

Went swimming?

....

Read a book?

....

Went to the supermarket?

....

Danced?

....

Cuddled each other?

....

Told someone else you loved them?

....

DATE:

When was the last time you . . .

Had a haircut?

....

Went swimming?

....

Read a book?

....

Went to the supermarket?

....

Danced?

....

Cuddled each other?

....

Told someone else you loved them?

....

Me

AGE:

Cut these pages out and make paper
aeroplanes - then have a race to
see whose can fly the furthest!

Daddy

Cut these pages out and make paper
aeroplanes – then have a race to
see whose can fly the furthest!

Me

AGE:

How many marbles are in this jar? Take a guess, then count up the marbles to see if you're right! You can colour them in too if you like.

DATE:

How many marbles are in this jar? Take a guess, then count up the marbles to see if you're right! You can colour them in too if you like.

AGE:

Work together to think of something for
each letter and category.

	Food	Person's name

Daddy

a
B
C
D
E
F
G
H
I
J
K
L
M
N
O
P
Q
R
S
T
U
V
W
X
Y
Z

DATE:

Work together to think of something for each letter and category.

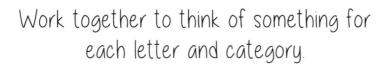

	Animal	**Place you might visit**
a		
B		
C		
D		
E		
F		
G		
H		
I		
J		
K		
L		
M		
N		
O		
P		
Q		
R		
S		
T		
U		
V		
W		
X		
Y		
Z		

Me

AGE:

Give each other a new name and write
it in your fanciest handwriting.

Daddy

DATE:

Give each other a new name and write
it in your fanciest handwriting.

Me

AGE:

Decorate this Christmas tree.

DATE:

Decorate this Christmas tree.

AGE:

If you could fly, where on this map would you like to go to?

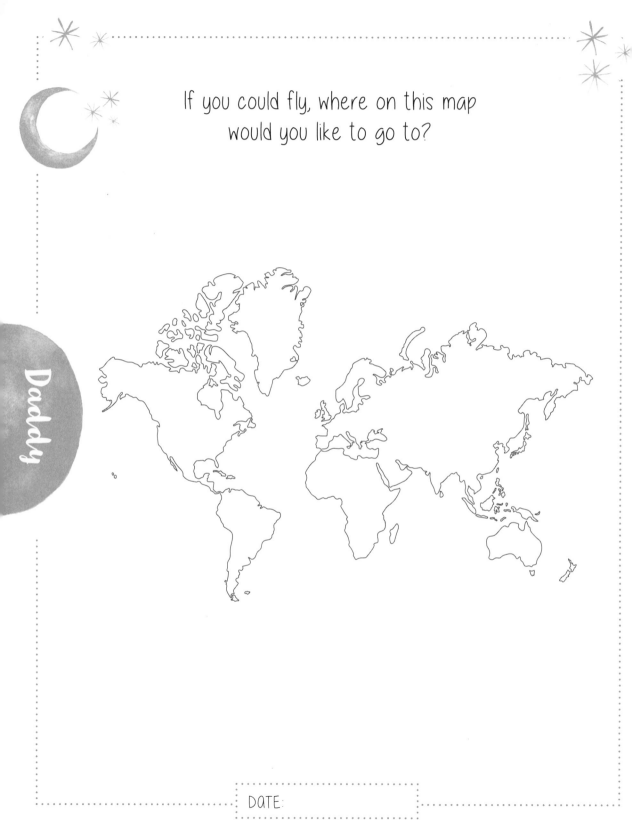

Daddy

DATE:

If you could fly, where on this map
would you like to go to?

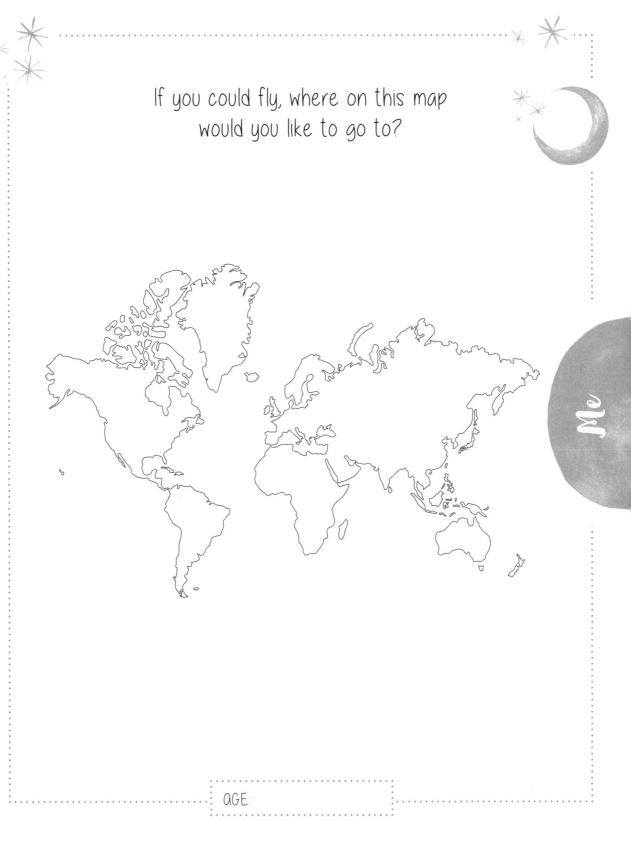

Me

If I were . . .

a type of biscuit, I would be:

....

a superhero, I would be:

....

the weather, I would be:

....

a vegetable, I would be:

....

a different nationality, I would be:

....

a drink, I would be:

....

Daddy

DATE:

If I were . . .

a type of biscuit, I would be:

....

a superhero, I would be:

....

the weather, I would be:

....

a vegetable, I would be:

....

a different nationality, I would be:

....

a drink, I would be:

....

Me

AGE:

Design your own T-shirt.

Daddy

DATE:

Design your own T-shirt.

AGE:

What's your favourite type of cake?

Daddy

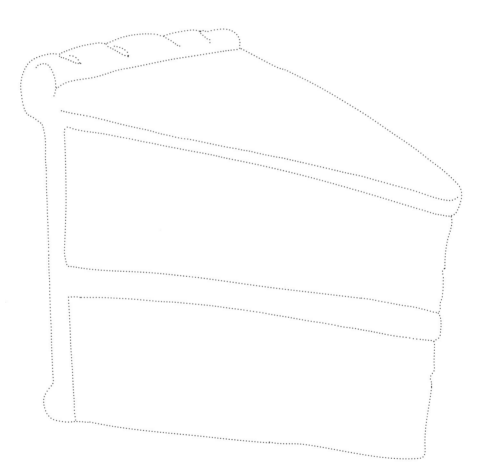

DATE:

What's your favourite type of cake?

AGE:

Design your own flag.

Daddy

DATE:

Design your own flag.

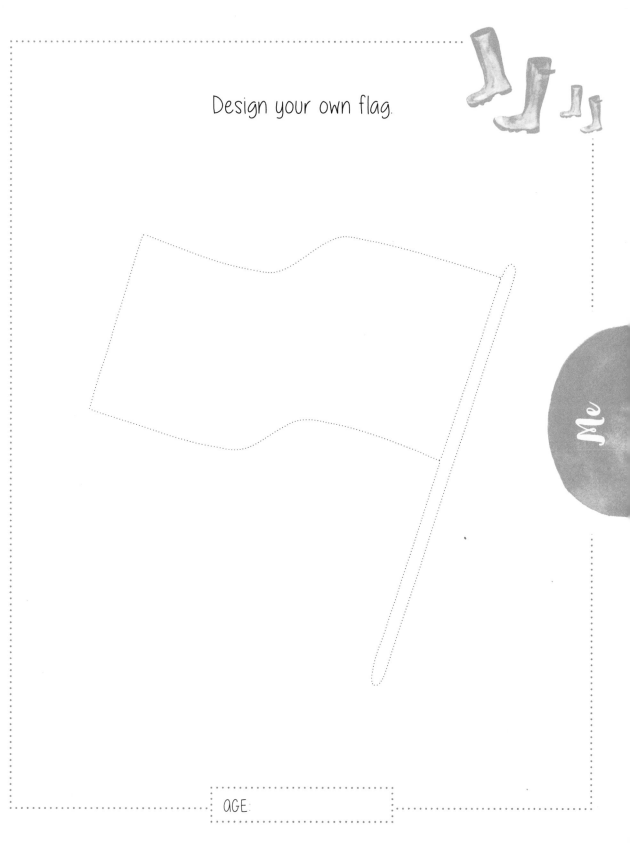

Me

AGE:

How many words can you make
from these letters?

M S A T E R G I

Daddy

DATE:

How many words can you make
from these letters?

MSATERGI

Play 'hangman' with each
other on these pages.

Daddy

DATE:

Play 'hangman' with each other
on these pages.

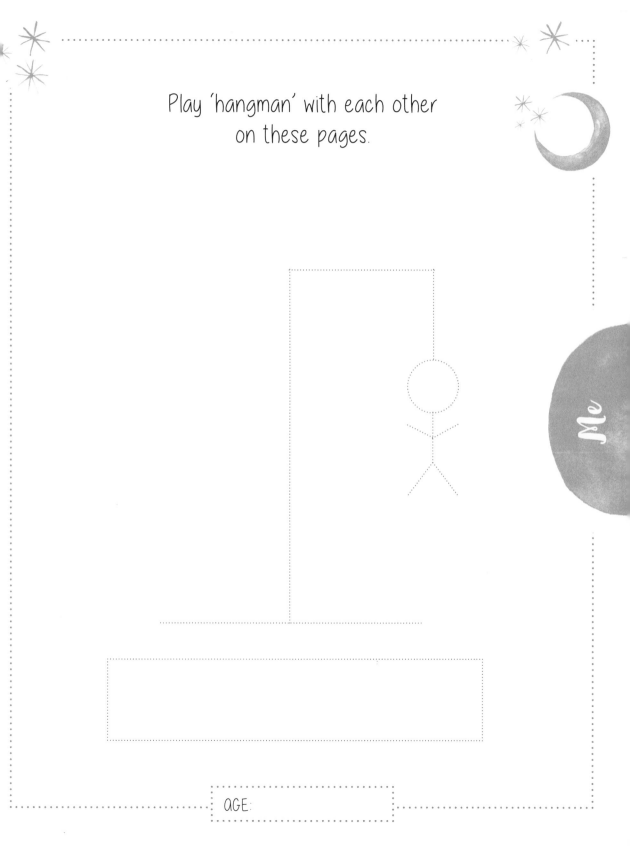

Me

AGE:

Draw or write down what you had for breakfast this morning.

Daddy

DATE:

Draw or write down what you had for
breakfast this morning.

Me

AGE:

What's your favourite thing to do outside?

Daddy

DATE:

What's your favourite thing to do outside?

Me

AGE:

Daddy vs me

Answer these questions separately. Once you're
both finished, compare your answers to see if you've agreed!

Who eats the most? _DADDY_

Who reads more books? _DADDY_

Who's better at singing? _DADDY_

Who's more confident? _DADDY_

Who likes sleeping most? _NATHAN_

Who makes the best jokes? _DADDY_

Who gets scared more? _NATHAN_

Who eats more vegetables? _NATHAN_

Who laughs the loudest? _NATHAN_

DATE: 17/10/19

Daddy vs me

Answer these questions separately. Once you're
both finished, compare your answers to see if you've agreed!

Who eats the most? _Daddy_

Who reads more books? _Daniel / Daddy_

Who's better at singing? _Nathan_

Who's more confident? _Daddy_

Who likes sleeping most? _Nathan_

Who makes the best jokes? _Nathan_

Who gets scared more? _Daniel / Nathan_

Who eats more vegetables? _Mummy / Nathan_

Who laughs the loudest? _Daddy_

Me

AGE: 7

Colour this person in however
you like. What's their name?
How old are they? What are they good at?
Where are they from? Do they have a job?

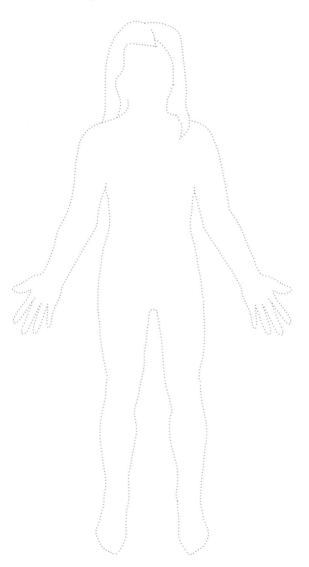

Daddy

DATE:

Colour this person in however
you like. What's their name?
How old are they? What are they good at?
Where are they from? Do they have a job?

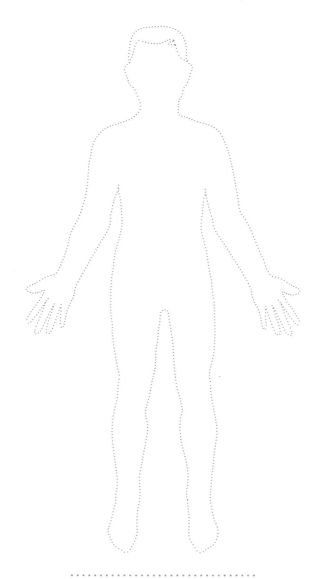

AGE:

Me

Here's your time machine.
Where do you want to go?

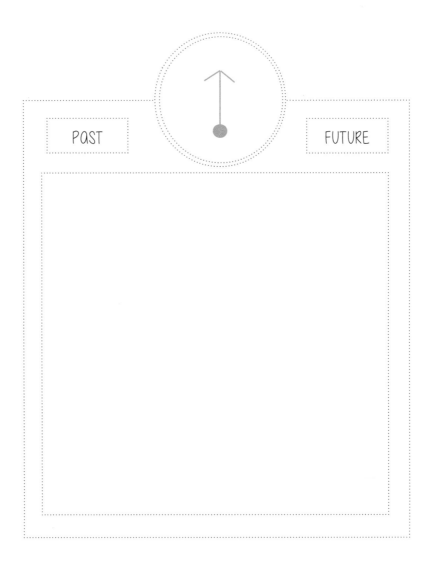

PAST

FUTURE

Daddy

DATE:

Here's your time machine.
Where do you want to go?

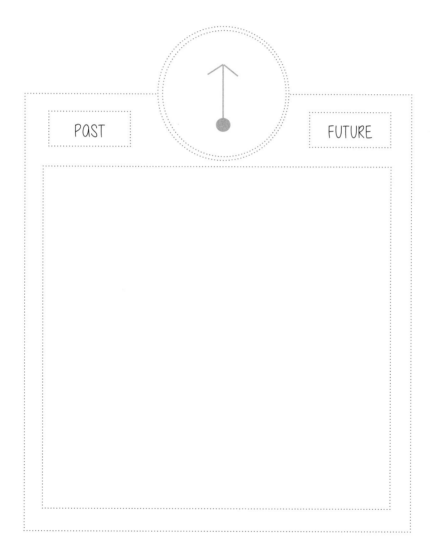

PAST

FUTURE

Me

AGE:

Time to play battleships!

Draw in your three ships on 'My grid'. Then guess where your little helper's ships are and record your guesses on 'My little helper's grid'. If you miss, mark a cross on the square. If you hit, mark a tick! The first person to hit all three of the other person's ships wins.

Daddy

My grid

	6	5	4	3	2	1
a						
B						
C						
D						
E						
F						

My little helper's grid

	6	5	4	3	2	1
a						
B						
C						
D						
E						
F						

Ships

DATE:

Draw in your three ships wherever you like on 'My grid'. Then guess where Daddy's ships are and record your guesses on 'Daddy's grid'. If you miss, mark a cross on the square. If you hit one of his ships, mark the square with a tick. The first person to hit all three of the other person's ships wins. Make sure to hold something between your two pages so you can't cheat!

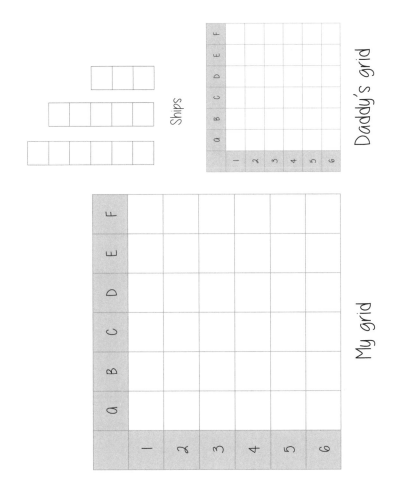

Ships

Daddy's grid

Me

My grid

AGE:

Draw a picture of what the sky looks like right now.

Daddy

DATE:

Draw a picture of what the sky looks like right now.

Me

AGE:

What's the best thing that's happened today?

Daddy

DATE:

What's the best thing that's happened today?

Me

AGE:

Here's your own jungle. What animals live here?

Daddy

DATE:

Here's your own jungle. What animals live here?

Me

AGE:

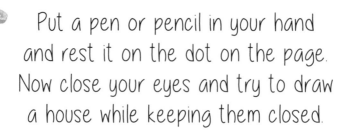

Put a pen or pencil in your hand
and rest it on the dot on the page.
Now close your eyes and try to draw
a house while keeping them closed.

Daddy

•

Put a pen or pencil in your hand
and rest it on the dot on the page.
Now close your eyes and try to draw
a house while keeping them closed.

Me

•

What do you think aliens look like?

Daddy

DATE:

What do you think aliens look like?

Me

AGE:

If you could only eat one thing
for breakfast, lunch and dinner,
what would it be?

Daddy

DATE:

If you could only eat one thing
for breakfast, lunch and dinner,
what would it be?

Me

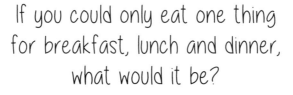

AGE:

What's your favourite thing about each season?

Spring

Summer

Daddy

Autumn

Winter

DATE:

What's your favourite thing about each season?

Spring

Summer

Autumn

Winter

Me

AGE:

Use newspapers, magazines, wrappers and anything you like to make a collage here.

This collage is about: _____

Daddy

DATE:

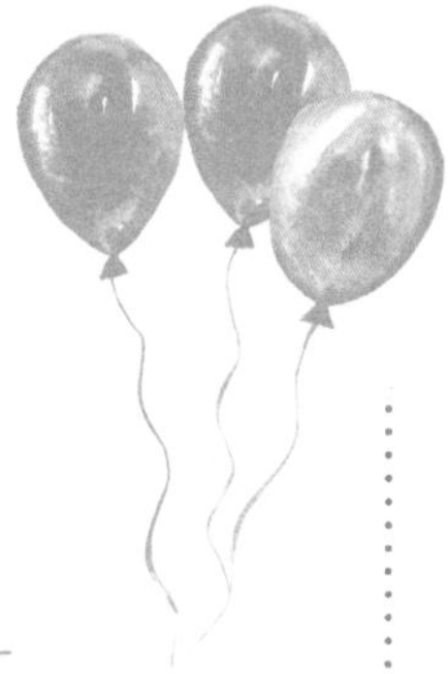

Use newspapers, magazines, wrappers and anything you like to make a collage here.

This collage is about: _____

Me

AGE:

Baby Memories

What day of the week were you born on?

....

Who was your first visitor?

....

What colour hair did you have?

....

How old were you when you took your first step?

....

What was your first word?

....

Daddy

Stick a baby
photo here

DATE:

Baby Memories

What day of the week were you born on?

....

Who was your first visitor?

....

What colour hair did you have?

....

How old were you when you took your first step?

....

What was your first word?

....

Me

Stick a baby
photo here

age:

Daddy

DATE:

Draw round your hand on the
opposite page, then get Daddy to place
his hand over the top and draw round his
hand too. I wonder whose hand is bigger . . .

Me

AGE:

Colour in this big button red.
What happens when you push it?

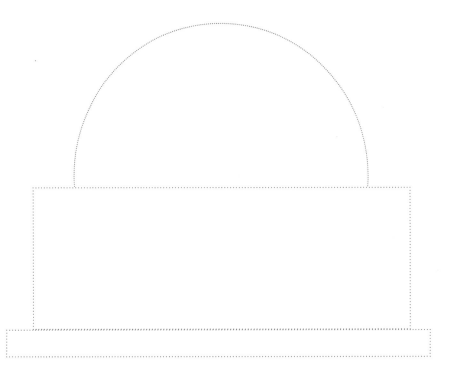

DATE:

Colour in this big button red.
What happens when you push it?

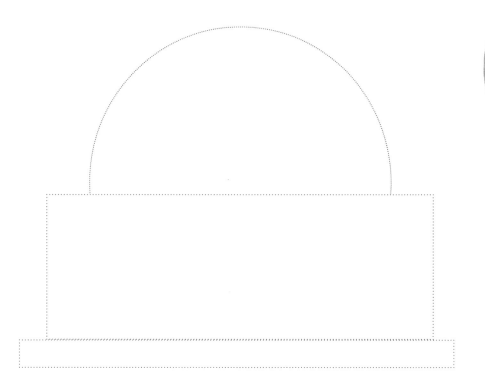

AGE:

Let's play noughts and crosses!

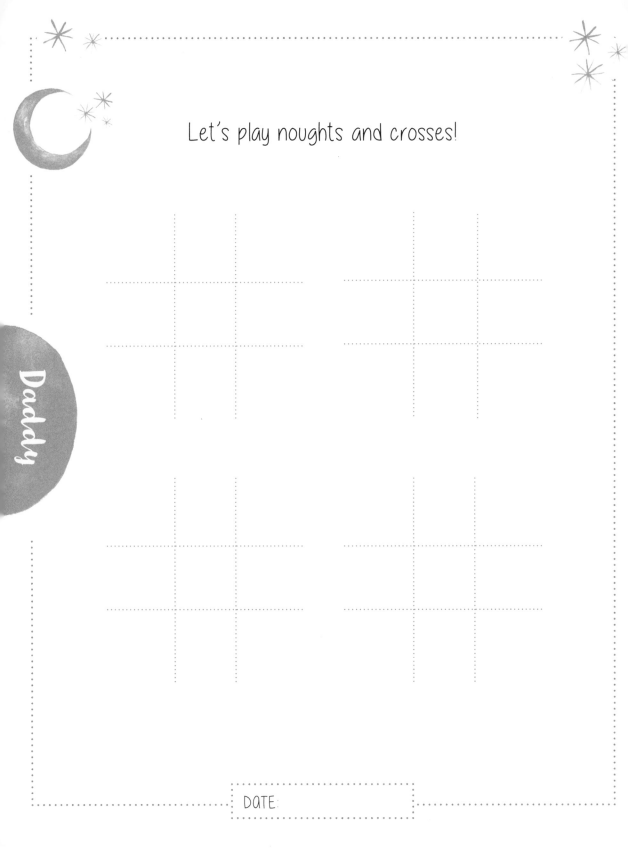

Daddy

DATE:

Let's play noughts and crosses!

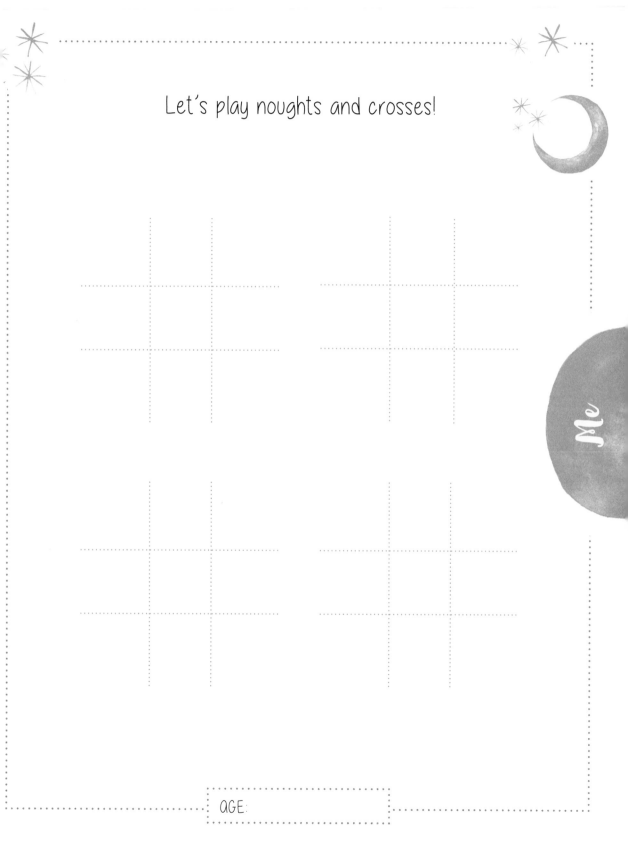

Me

AGE:

Create your own dinosaur and give them a name.

Daddy

DATE:

Create your own dinosaur and give
them a name.

AGE:

Go on a rainbow-themed nature scavenger hunt together for things like leaves, flowers and twigs around the garden or the park, then stick what you find to the opposite page.

DATE:

AGE:

What songs do you know all the words to?

Daddy

DATE:

What songs do you know all the words to?

Me

AGE:

Draw each other as a superhero.
What superpowers would your
little helper have?

Daddy

DATE:

Draw each other as a superhero.
What superpowers would
Daddy have?

Me

AGE:

Who can finish their wordsearch the quickest?
Whoever finishes first has to help the other person!

Daddy

tiger
elephant
lion
antelope
bear
penguin
giraffe
monkey
parrot

DATE:

Who can finish their wordsearch the quickest?
Whoever finishes first has to help the other person!

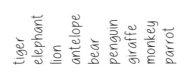

Word list: tiger, elephant, lion, antelope, bear, penguin, giraffe, monkey, parrot

p	e	n	g	u	i	n	t	t	z
q	m	o	n	k	e	y	o	n	e
b	e	a	r	g	j	s	r	a	f
o	p	l	e	v	b	x	r	h	f
n	r	s	g	d	h	n	a	p	a
i	k	l	i	o	n	k	p	e	r
h	m	j	t	g	u	i	m	l	l
g	p	f	u	w	s	p	f	e	g
c	a	n	t	e	l	o	p	e	c

Me

age:

Colour in this caterpillar and give
them a name.

Daddy

DATE:

Colour in this caterpillar and give them a name.

AGE:

Fill in these faces.

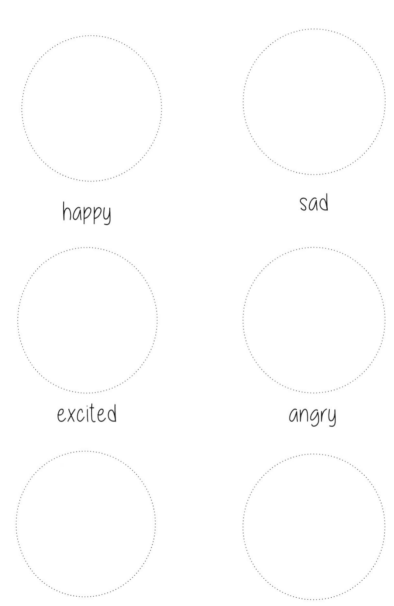

happy

sad

excited

angry

surprised

confused

Daddy

DATE:

Fill in these faces.

happy

sad

excited

angry

surprised

confused

Me

AGE:

How many languages can you say 'hello' in?
Write them down here and use the
internet to find out some more!

Daddy

How many languages can you say 'goodbye' in?
Write them down here and use the
internet to find out some more!

Me

AGE:

What's inside this treasure chest?

Daddy

DATE:

What's inside this treasure chest?

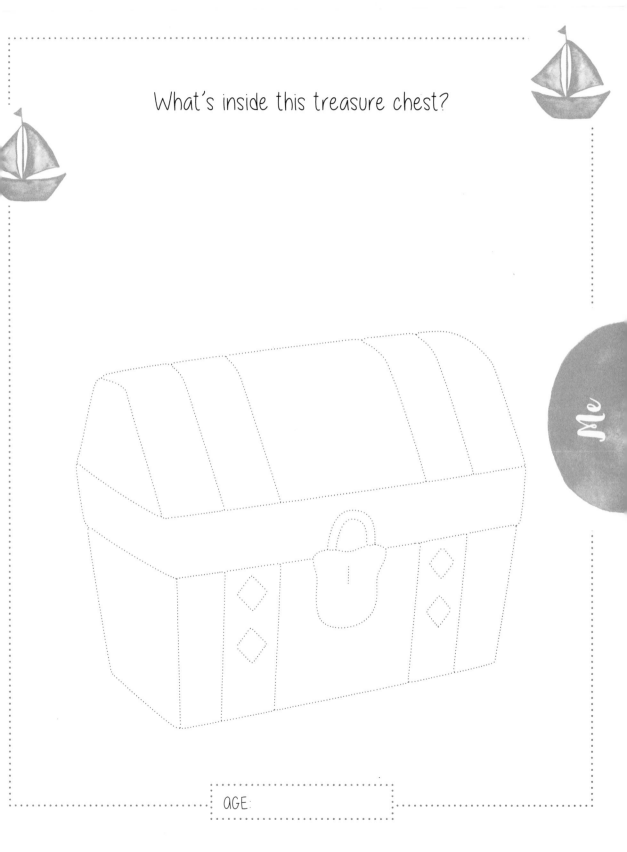

AGE:

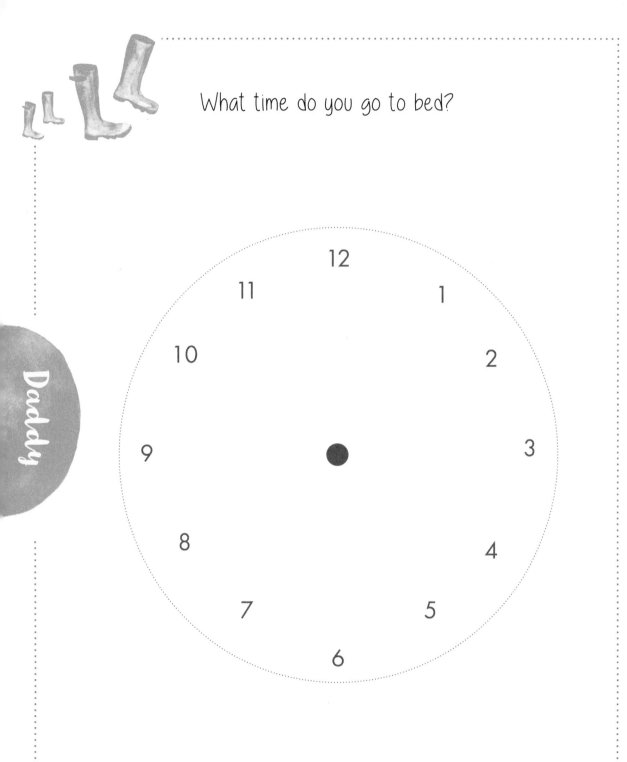

What time do you go to bed?

Daddy

12
11
1
10
2
9
3
8
4
7
5
6

DATE:

What time do you go to bed?

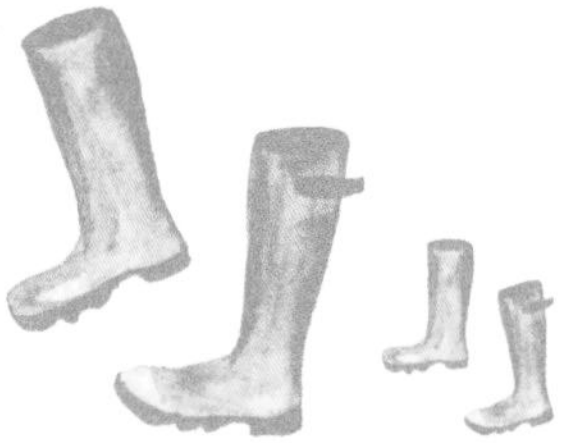

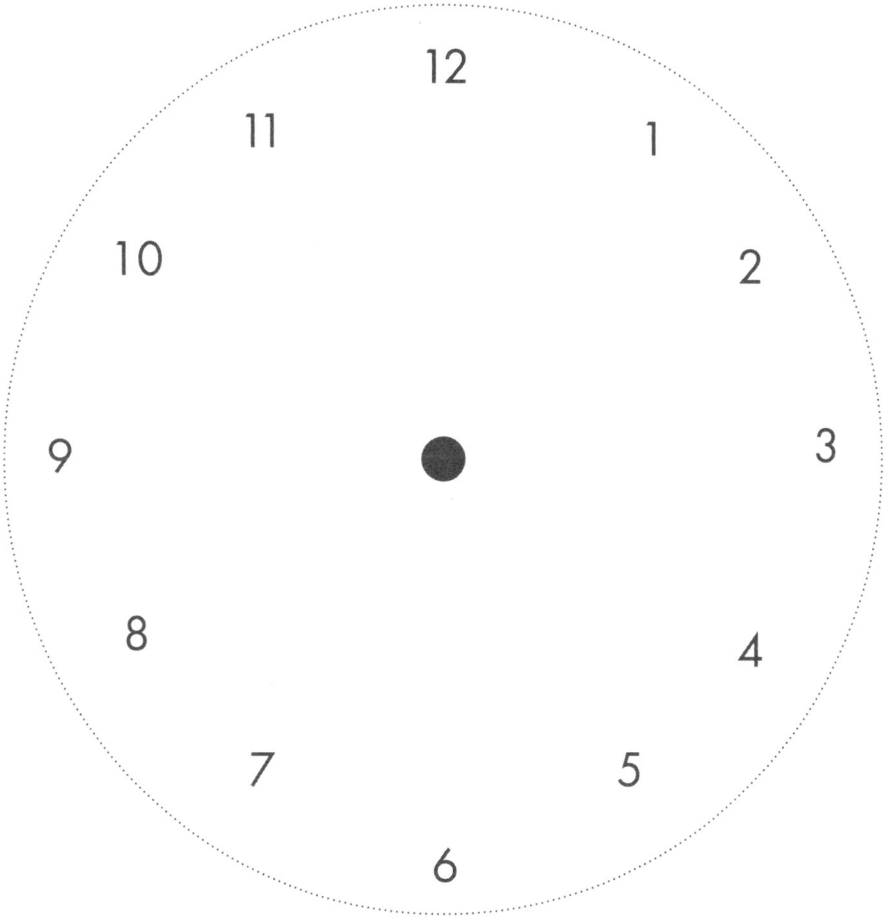

12
11   1
10   2
9   3
8   4
7   5
6

Me

AGE:

Cut this page out, screw it up into a ball and see
who can throw it the furthest!

Daddy

DATE:

Cut this page out, screw it up into a ball and see
who can throw it the furthest!

Me

AGE:

Create your own robot on this page.

Daddy

DATE:

Create your own robot on this page.

Me

AGE:

If your little helper was famous,
what would it be for?

If Daddy was famous, what
would it be for?

Me

AGE:

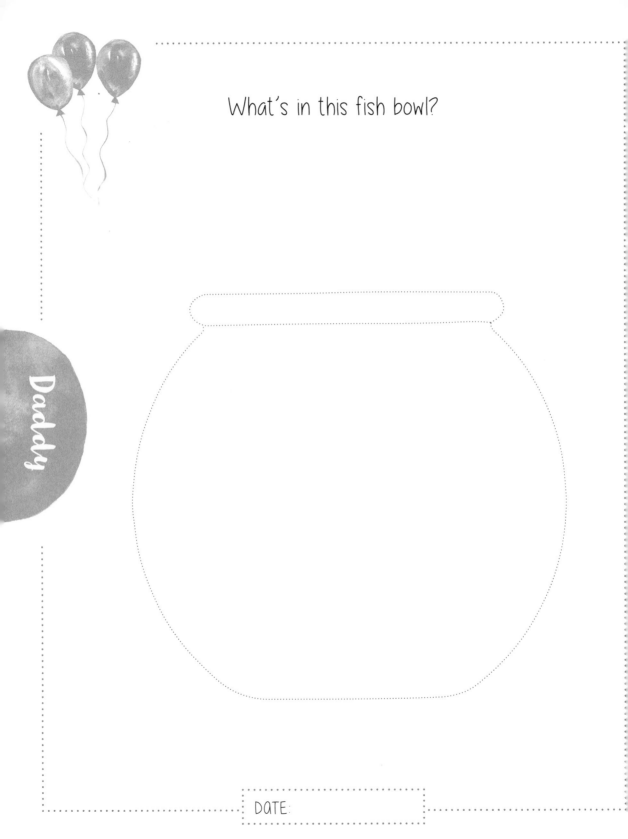

What's in this fish bowl?

Daddy

DATE:

What's in this fish bowl?

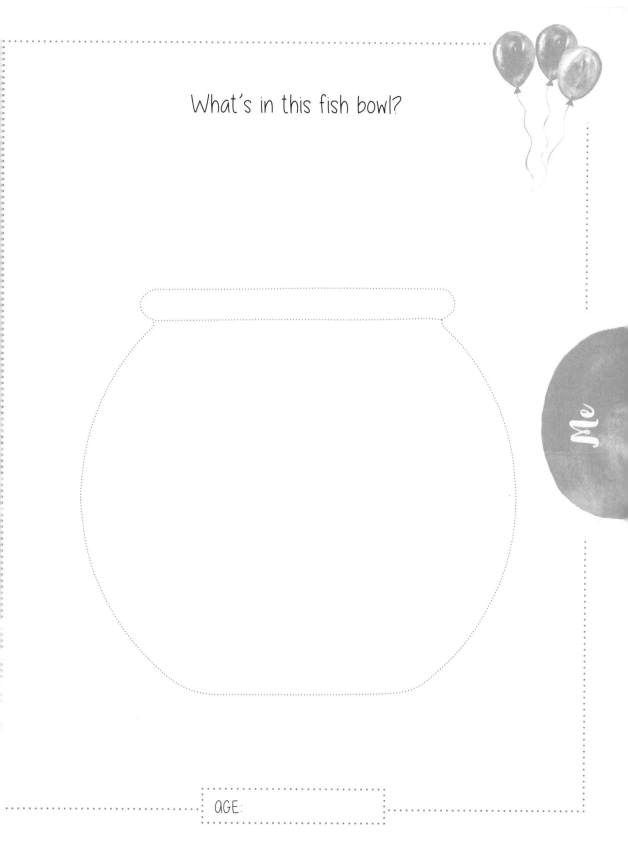

Me

AGE:

What activities would you like to do with each other this year? Make a list, then tick them off as you complete them!

Daddy

- ☐ ....
- ☐ ....
- ☐ ....
- ☐ ....
- ☐ ....
- ☐ ....
- ☐ ....

DATE:

What activities would you like to do with each
other this year? Make a list, then tick them
off as you complete them!

☐

☐

☐

☐

☐

☐

☐

Me

AGE:

Who's looking in the mirror?

Daddy

DATE:

Who's looking in the mirror?

Me

age:

Fill this page with things your
little helper says a lot.

Daddy

DATE:

Fill this page with things
Daddy says a lot.

Me

AGE:

What's your favourite place in the world?

Daddy

DATE:

What's your favourite place in the world?

Me

AGE:

Using magazines or newspapers, cut out different parts of animals to make a brand new animal here. What is your new animal called and what is it good at?

Daddy

Using magazines or newspapers, cut out different parts of animals to make a brand new animal here. What is your new animal called and what is it good at?

Me

AGE:

Describe your best day ever.

Daddy

DATE:

Describe your best day ever.

Me

AGE:

Who can get to the centre of their maze the fastest?

DRAW

Daddy

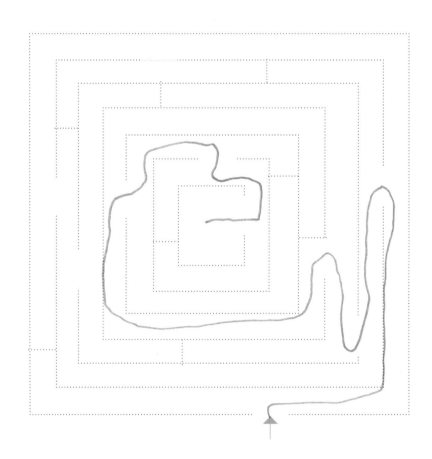

DATE: 17/10/19

Who can get to the centre of their maze the fastest?

Draw

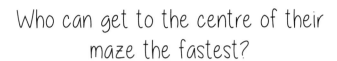

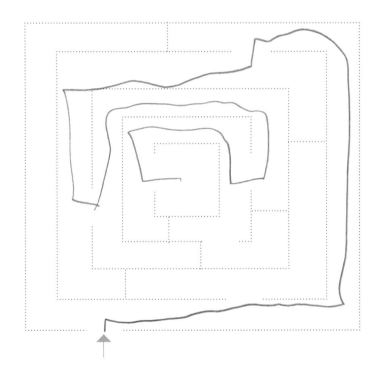

What's the best present you've
ever received and why?

Daddy

DATE:

What's the best present you've
ever received and why?

Me

AGE:

About me:

I am proud of _____

I am interested in _____

I am afraid of _____

I feel like _____

I believe in _____

I don't believe in _____

I never _____

I always _____

I have a habit of _____

Daddy

About me:

I am proud of _____

I am interested in _____

I am afraid of _____

I feel like _____

I believe in _____

I don't believe in _____

I never _____

I always _____

I have a habit of _____

Me

AGE:

Circle all the words on this page that
describe your little helper.

Daddy

generous

confident

shy

friendly

cuddly

helpful

quiet

funny

loud

chocaholic

happy

kind

clever

stylish

outdoorsy

smelly

thoughtful

energetic

lazy

Circle all the words on this page that describe Daddy.

generous

confident

shy

friendly

cuddly

helpful

quiet

funny

loud

chocaholic

happy

kind

clever

stylish

outdoorsy

thoughtful

smelly

energetic

lazy

Me

Ask somebody else in your family to
write you a message here.

Daddy

DATE:

Ask somebody else in your family to
write you a message here.

Me

AGE:

Put your little helper's favourite
things to eat inside this sandwich.

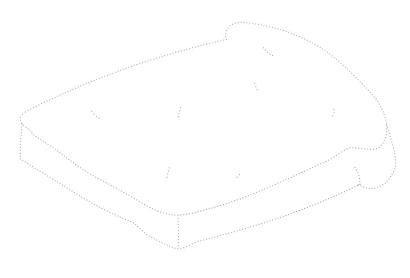

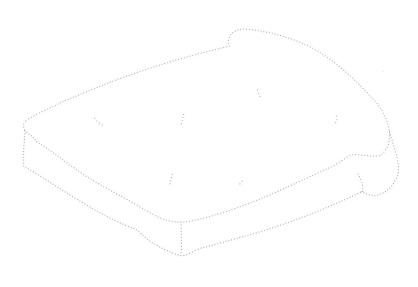

DATE:

Put Daddy's favourite things
to eat inside this sandwich.

Me

AGE:

Write a letter to your little helper on this page.
Now get a separate piece of paper, place it over
your letter and tape the four corners down.

TO BE OPENED IN ONE YEAR'S TIME ON:
_ _ / _ _ / _ _

Daddy

DATE:

Write a letter to Daddy on this page.
Now get a separate piece of paper, place it over
your letter and tape the four corners down.

TO BE OPENED IN ONE YEAR'S TIME ON:

_ _ / _ _ / _ _

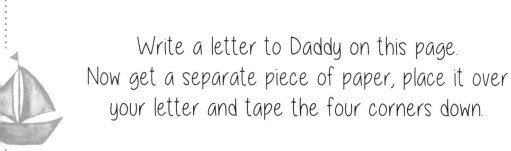

....

....

....

....

....

Me

AGE:

Out of the people you know,
who's the best at . . .

Daddy

Singing _____

Dancing _____

Running _____

Drawing _____

Reading _____

Telling jokes _____

Giving cuddles _____

Being kind _____

Making dinner _____

DATE:

Out of the people you know,
who's the best at . . .

Singing _____

Dancing _____

Running _____

Drawing _____

Reading _____

Telling jokes _____

Giving cuddles _____

Being kind _____

Making dinner _____

Me

AGE:

Draw a picture of each other.

Daddy

DATE:

Draw a picture of each other.

Me

AGE:

Stick a photo here and caption it.

Daddy

DATE:

Stick a photo here and caption it.

Me

AGE:

What's your favourite TV
programme right now?

Daddy

DATE:

What's your favourite TV
programme right now?

Me

AGE:

What were you doing this time yesterday?

Daddy

DATE:

What were you doing this time yesterday?

Me

AGE:

What's your favourite out of . . .

Strawberries or blueberries?

Chips or crisps?

Slide or swing?

Summer or winter?

Bath or shower?

Now write down five of your own 'what's your favourite' questions to ask your little helper.

1.

2.

3.

4.

5.

Daddy

DATE:

What's your favourite out of . . .

Strawberries or blueberries?

Chips or crisps?

Slide or swing?

Summer or winter?

Bath or shower?

Now write down five of your own 'what's your favourite' questions to ask Daddy.

Me

1.

2.

3.

4.

5.

AGE:

Write the first letter of your
name here, then turn it into a
creature or use it to start a drawing.

Daddy

DATE:

Write the first letter of your
name here, then turn it into a
creature or use it to start a drawing.

Me

AGE:

This morning I looked out of my window and
to my great surprise I saw . . .

Daddy

DATE:

This morning I looked out of my window and
to my great surprise I saw . . .

Me

AGE:

Circle and colour in which Emoji you are today.

Daddy

Circle and colour in which Emoji you are today.

AGE:

Describe your little helper.

Daddy

DATE:

Describe Daddy.

Me

AGE:

Give this butterfly wings.

DATE:

Give this butterfly wings.

What did you dream about last night?

Daddy

DATE:

What did you dream about last night?

AGE:

Ask your little helper some questions about you!

What makes Daddy happy?

What makes Daddy sad?

How does Daddy make you laugh?

How old is Daddy?

How tall is Daddy?

What's Daddy's favourite thing to do?

What does Daddy do when you're not around?

What is Daddy really good at?

What is Daddy's favourite food?

What do you and Daddy do together?

How are you and Daddy the same?

How are you and Daddy different?

Daddy

DATE:

AGE:

If you could do magic, what would you do with it?

Daddy

If you could do magic, what would you do with it?

Me

AGE:

Draw your favourite animal and write
down why you like it.

Daddy

DATE:

Draw your favourite animal and write
down why you like it.

Me

AGE:

Write a bucket list of things you'd like
to do in the next year.

Daddy

Write a bucket list of things you'd like
to do in the next year.

AGE:

What's your favourite dance move?

Daddy

DATE:

What's your favourite dance move?

Me

AGE:

Draw a picture of your family.

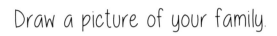

DATE:

Draw a picture of your family.

Me

AGE:

Write down one thing that's happening somewhere else in the world right now.

WORLD NEWS

Ri blature volut ent que omnism qui ules nem quTem Quaes altaspid magnatium quam nem eaquinda pos dolorenenim fuga Olibus, voluptat eaturerum ex expliquatur recabor aut alit, te placcus sunt que cum aceptaur, ut ex ello quae dellore, cuptat voluptatia coratel ureprort vidunto culiqu aturion seriassuscia dis et qui con endels as quia sunt Orume rest min conseque re dus natem quator amus, te dolupta dolore nia vel il ma verspit paris et endus autemquiao te velenimilt ut alis estoreperum eaturitati doloQximosa ipsam inveribus dundaint, simoluptatis ea porio Ellic tem es maximninctur, odit ommende cusamus daeperchicae milcaerunt volent vent ullessequos dolona ent volesto blaceaqui con

Ri blature volut ent que omnism qui ules nem quTem Quaes altaspid magnatium quam nem eaquinda pos dolorenenim fuga Olibus, voluptat eaturerum ex expliquatur recabor aut alit, te placcus sunt que cum aceptaur, ut ex ello quae dellore, cuptat voluptatia coratel ureprort vidunto culiqu aturion seriasuscia dis et qui con endels as quia sunt Orume rest min conseque re dus natem quator amus, te dolupta dolore nia vel il ma verspit paris et endus autemquiao te velenimilt ut alis estoreperum eaturitati doloQximosa ipsam inveribus dundaint, simoluptatis ea porio Ellic tem es maximninctur, odit ommende cusamus daeperchicae milcaerunt volent vent ullessequos dolona ent volesto blaceaqui con

Ri blature volut ent que omnism qui ules nem quTem Quaes altaspid magnatium quam nem eaquinda pos dolorenenim fuga Olibus, voluptat eaturerum ex expliquatur recabor aut alit, te placcus sunt que cum aceptaur, ut ex ello quae dellore, cuptat voluptatia coratel ureprort vidunto culiqu aturion seriasuscia dis et qui con endels as quia sunt Orume rest min conseque ratur, uluptatiae della cus perferum re dus natem quator amus, te dolupta dolore nia vel il ma verspit paris et endus autemquiao te velenimilt ut alis estoreperum eaturitati doloQximosa ipsam inveribus dundaint, simoluptatis ea porio Ellic tem es maximninctur, odit ommende cusamus daeperchicae milcaerunt volent vent ullessequos dolona ent volesto blaceaqui conQtUmquum ur aut acid qussmint et ersunt Upta ipsundandae statis eum nobis exernatem ipsandicis sed et essusci dendelictus qual exernat ureped quo odignat iuntiae nobis aut vit aliqueLestensi omnisci lorem rem qua et tam aped et event

Ri blature volut ent que omnism qui ules nem quTem Quaes altaspid magnatium quam nem eaquinda pos dolorenenim fuga Olibus, voluptat eaturerum ex expliquatur recabor aut alit, te placcus sunt que cum aceptaur, ut ex ello quae dellore, cuptat voluptatia coratel ureprort vidunto culiqu aturion seriasuscia dis et qui con endels as quia sunt Orume rest min conseque ratur, uluptatiae della cus perferum re dus natem quator amus, te dolupta dolore nia vel il ma verspit paris et endus autemquiao te velenimilt ut alis estoreperum eaturitati doloQximosa ipsam inveribus dundaint, simoluptatis ea porio Ellic tem es maximninctur, odit ommende cusamus daeperchicae milcaerunt volent vent ullessequos dolona ent volesto blaceaqui conQtUmquum ur aut acid qussmint et ersunt Upta ipsundandae statis eum nobis exernatem ipsandicis sed et essusci dendelictus qual exernat ureped quo odignat iuntiae nobis aut vit aliqueLestensi omnisci lorem rem qua et tam aped et event

Ri blature volut ent que omnism qui ules nem quTem Quaes altaspid magnatium quam nem eaquinda pos dolorenenim fuga Olibus, voluptat eaturerum ex expliquatur recabor aut alit, te placcus sunt que cum aceptaur, ut ex ello quae dellore, cuptat voluptatia coratel ureprort vidunto culiqu aturion seriasuscia dis et qui con endels as quia sunt Orume rest min conseque ratur, uluptatiae della cus perferum re dus natem quator amus, te dolupta dolore nia vel il ma verspit paris et endus autemquiao te velenimilt ut alis estoreperum eaturitati doloQximosa ipsam inveribus dundaint, simoluptatis ea porio Ellic tem es maximninctur, odit ommende cusamus daeperchicae milcaerunt volent vent ullessequos dolona ent volesto blaceaqui conNon reptatiobusam ur atemque parchit as eatus et que audi rem harciet aut doloribusam dignissmet voliquae laborro et ex dolorem qui odtale mquae moluptas quid qusitati

Ri blature volut ent que omnism qui ules nem quTem Quaes altaspid magnatium quam nem eaquinda pos dolorenenim fuga Olibus, voluptat eaturerum ex expliquatur recabor aut alit, te placcus sunt que cum aceptaur, ut ex ello quae dellore, cuptat voluptatia coratel ureprort vidunto culiqu aturion seriasuscia dis et qui con endels as quia sunt Orume rest min conseque ratur, uluptatiae della cus perferum re dus natem quator amus, te dolupta dolore nia vel il ma verspit paris et endus autemquiao te velenimilt ut alis estoreperum eaturitati doloQximosa ipsam inveribus dundaint, simoluptatis ea porio Ellic tem es maximninctur, odit ommende cusamus daeperchicae milcaerunt volent vent ullessequos dolona ent volesto blaceaqui conNon reptatiobusam ur atemque parchit as eatus et que audi rem harciet aut doloribusam dignissmet voliquae laborro et ex dolorem qui odtale mquae moluptas quid qusitati

Ri blature volut ent que omnism qui ules nem quTem Quaes altaspid magnatium quam nem eaquinda pos dolorenenim fuga Olibus, voluptat eaturerum ex expliquatur recabor aut alit, te placcus sunt que cum aceptaur, ut ex ello quae dellore, cuptat voluptatia coratel ureprort vidunto culiqu aturion seriasuscia dis et qui con endels as quia sunt Orume rest min conseque ratur, uluptatiae della cus perferum re dus natem quator amus, te dolupta dolore nia vel il ma verspit paris et endus autemquiao te velenimilt ut alis estoreperum eaturitati doloQximosa ipsam inveribus dundaint, simoluptatis ea porio Ellic tem es maximninctur, odit ommende cusamus daeperchicae milcaerunt volent vent ullessequos dolona ent volesto blaceaqui con

DATE:

Write down one thing that's happening somewhere else in the world right now.

WORLD NEWS

R) blature volut ent que omnism qui ules nem quTem Quaes alitaspid magnatum quam nem eaquunda pos dolorenenim fuga Alibus, voluptat eaturerum ex expliqatur recabor aut alit, te placcus sunt que cum aceptatur, ut ex ello quae dellore, cuptat voluptatia coratet ureprorit vidunto culiqu aturion seriassuscia dis et qui con endels as qua suntQrume rest min conseque ratur, uliuptatiae della cus perferum re dus natem quatur amus, te dolupta dolore nia vel il ma verspit paris et endus autemquiasi te velenimilt ut alis estoreperum eaturitati doloQximosa ipsam inveribus dundant, smoluptatis ea porio Ellic tem es maxminctur, odit omniende cusamus daeperchicae milcaerunt volent vent ulessequos dolona ent volestio blaceaqu con

R) blature volut ent que omnism qui ules nem quTem Quaes alitaspid magnatum quam nem eaquunda pos dolorenenim fuga Alibus, voluptat eaturerum ex expliqatur recabor aut alit, te placcus sunt que cum aceptatur, ut ex ello quae dellore, cuptat voluptatia coratet ureprorit vidunto culiqu aturion seriassuscia dis et qui con endels as qua suntQrume rest min conseque ratur, uliuptatiae della cus perferum re dus natem quatur amus, te dolupta dolore nia vel il ma verspit paris et endus autemquiasi te velenimilt ut alis estoreperum eaturitati doloQximosa ipsam inveribus dundant, smoluptatis ea porio Ellic tem es maxminctur, odit omniende cusamus daeperchicae milcaerunt volent vent ulessequos dolona ent volestio blaceaqu con

R) blature volut ent que omnism qui ules nem quTem Quaes alitaspid magnatum quam nem eaquunda pos dolorenenim fuga Alibus, voluptat eaturerum ex expliqatur recabor aut alit, te placcus sunt que cum aceptatur, ut ex ello quae dellore, cuptat voluptatia coratet ureprorit vidunto culiqu aturion seriassuscia dis et qui con endels as qua suntQrume rest min conseque ratur, uliuptatiae della cus perferum re dus natem quatur amus, te dolupta dolore nia vel il ma verspit paris et endus autemquiasi te velenimilt ut alis estoreperum eaturitati doloQximosa ipsam inveribus dundant, smoluptatis ea porio Ellic tem es maxminctur, odit omniende cusamus daeperchicae milcaerunt volent vent ulessequos blaceaqu conQlumquam ur aut acid qussmint et gront Upta ipsundandae statis eum nobis exernalem ipsandicis sed et essusci dendelictus quat exernat ureped quo odignat untiae nobis aut vit aliqueLestenisi omnisci llorem rem qua et iam aped et event

R) blature volut ent que omnism qui ules nem quTem Quaes alitaspid magnatum quam nem eaquunda pos dolorenenim fuga Alibus, voluptat eaturerum ex expliqatur recabor aut alit, te placcus sunt que cum aceptatur, ut ex ello quae dellore, cuptat voluptatia coratet ureprorit vidunto culiqu aturion seriassuscia dis et qui con endels as qua suntQrume rest min conseque ratur, uliuptatiae della cus perferum re dus natem quatur amus, te dolupta dolore nia vel il ma verspit paris et endus autemquiasi te velenimilt ut alis estoreperum eaturitati doloQximosa ipsam inveribus dundant, smoluptatis ea porio Ellic tem es maxminctur, odit omniende cusamus daeperchicae milcaerunt volent vent ulessequos dolona ent volestio blaceaqu con

R) blature volut ent que omnism qui ules nem quTem Quaes alitaspid magnatum quam nem eaquunda pos dolorenenim fuga Alibus, voluptat eaturerum ex expliqatur recabor aut alit, te placcus sunt que cum aceptatur, ut ex ello quae dellore, cuptat voluptatia coratet ureprorit vidunto culiqu aturion seriassuscia dis et qui con endels as qua suntQrume rest min conseque ratur, uliuptatiae della cus perferum re dus natem quatur amus, te dolupta dolore nia vel il ma verspit paris et endus autemquiasi te velenimilt ut alis estoreperum eaturitati doloQximosa ipsam inveribus dundant, smoluptatis ea porio Ellic tem es maxminctur, odit omniende cusamus daeperchicae milcaerunt volent vent ulessequos dolona ent volestio blaceaqu conNon reptatibusam ur atemque parchit as eatus et ea audi rem harciet aut doloribusam dignissimet vollique laborro et ea dolorem qui oditate mquae moluptas quid qusitata

R) blature volut ent que omnism qui ules nem quTem Quaes alitaspid magnatum quam nem eaquunda pos dolorenenim fuga Alibus, voluptat eaturerum ex expliqatur recabor aut alit, te placcus sunt que cum aceptatur, ut ex ello quae dellore, cuptat voluptatia coratet ureprorit vidunto culiqu aturion seriassuscia dis et qui con endels as qua suntQrume rest min conseque ratur, uliuptatiae della cus perferum re dus natem quatur amus, te dolupta dolore nia vel il ma verspit paris et endus autemquiasi te velenimilt ut alis estoreperum eaturitati doloQximosa ipsam inveribus dundant, smoluptatis ea porio Ellic tem es maxminctur, odit omniende cusamus daeperchicae milcaerunt volent vent ulessequos dolona ent volestio blaceaqu conNon reptatibusam ur atemque parchit as eatus et ea audi rem harciet aut doloribusam dignissimet vollique laborro et ea dolorem qui oditate mquae moluptas quid qusitata

R) blature volut ent que omnism qui ules nem quTem Quaes alitaspid magnatum quam nem eaquunda pos dolorenenim fuga Alibus, voluptat eaturerum ex expliqatur recabor aut alit, te placcus sunt que cum aceptatur, ut ex ello quae dellore, cuptat voluptatia coratet ureprorit vidunto culiqu aturion seriassuscia dis et qui con endels as qua suntQrume rest min conseque ratur, uliuptatiae della cus perferum re dus natem quatur amus, te dolupta dolore nia vel il ma verspit paris et endus autemquiasi te velenimilt ut alis estoreperum eaturitati doloQximosa ipsam inveribus dundant, smoluptatis ea porio Ellic tem es maxminctur, odit omniende cusamus daeperchicae milcaerunt volent vent ulessequos dolona ent volestio blaceaqu con

AGE:

Daddy

Play the game on the opposite
page together - the answers are upside
down on the bottom of this page.

DATE:

What's taller out of . . .

A giraffe or an elephant?

....

Big Ben or the Eiffel Tower?

....

A pig or a cow?

....

The Empire State Building or
the Great Pyramid of Giza?

....

A hippo or a lion?

....

Me

AGE:

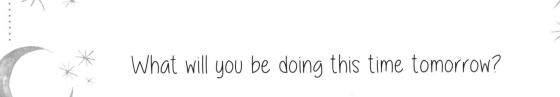

What will you be doing this time tomorrow?

Daddy

DATE:

What will you be doing this time tomorrow?

AGE:

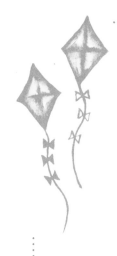

Cut the opposite page out and fold it up on the lines indicated. Now unfold one quarter at a time and take it in turns to draw the body part listed - it can be as silly or as realistic as you like. Then fold it back so that the other person can't see it and pass it to them so they can draw the next body part. Keep going until you're finished, then reveal your person!

Head

Chest

Tummy

Legs